T0109484

Published in the U.S. by:
ULYSSES PRESS
P.O. Box 3440
Berkeley, CA 94703
www.ulyssespress.com

ISBN: 978-1-64604-043-8
Library of Congress Control Number: 2020931855

Printed in Korea by Artin Printing Company through Four Colour Print Group
10 9 8 7 6 5 4 3 2 1

Acquisitions editor: Casie Vogel
Managing editor: Claire Chun
Editor: Renee Rutledge
Proofreader: Miriam Jones
Cover design: what!design @ whatweb.com
Cover photograph: © Javier Brosch/shutterstock.com
Interior design: Jake Flaherty
Interior photographs: © shutterstock.com; page 3 © Katrina Brown; page 6 © Olist; page 9 © Buy This; page 10, 46 © Monkey Business Images; page 13 © Masarik; page 14 © Istvan Csak; page 17, 45 © Javier Brosch; page 18 © Aleksey Boyko; page 21 © Masarik; page 22 © Monika Wisniewska; page 25 © Dan Smith Photography; page 26 © Sundays Photography; page 29 © KristinaSh; page 30 © Daniela Breznova; page 33 © Aneta Jungerova; page 34 © Kuznetsov Alexey; page 37 © Darina Matasova; page 38 © alexei_tm; page 41 © Linn Currie; page 42 © KikoStock; page 49 © Wasitt Hemwarapornchai; page 50 © Jolanta Beinarovica; page 53 © ValSN; page 54 © Tatiana Zinchenko; page 57 © PardoY; page 58 © StockMediaSeller; page 61 © Christine Wilson Photos; page 62 © mj-tim photography

Wishing You a Very Happy Retirement!

Congratulations! Say goodbye to the daily grind and get down to the real work: retirement.

It's your time to hit the golf course, soak up the sun, whip out your AARP card, enjoy those coveted senior discounts, and—of course—celebrate the best years of your life!

There are no more grumpy bosses to tell you what to do...

...instead it's your chance to chart your own course!

No more carpal tunnel...

...more like carpe diem!

Stop dreaming about taking a nap at work...

...and start living

the dream!

Avoid the afternoon slump...

...and make every
afternoon happy hour!

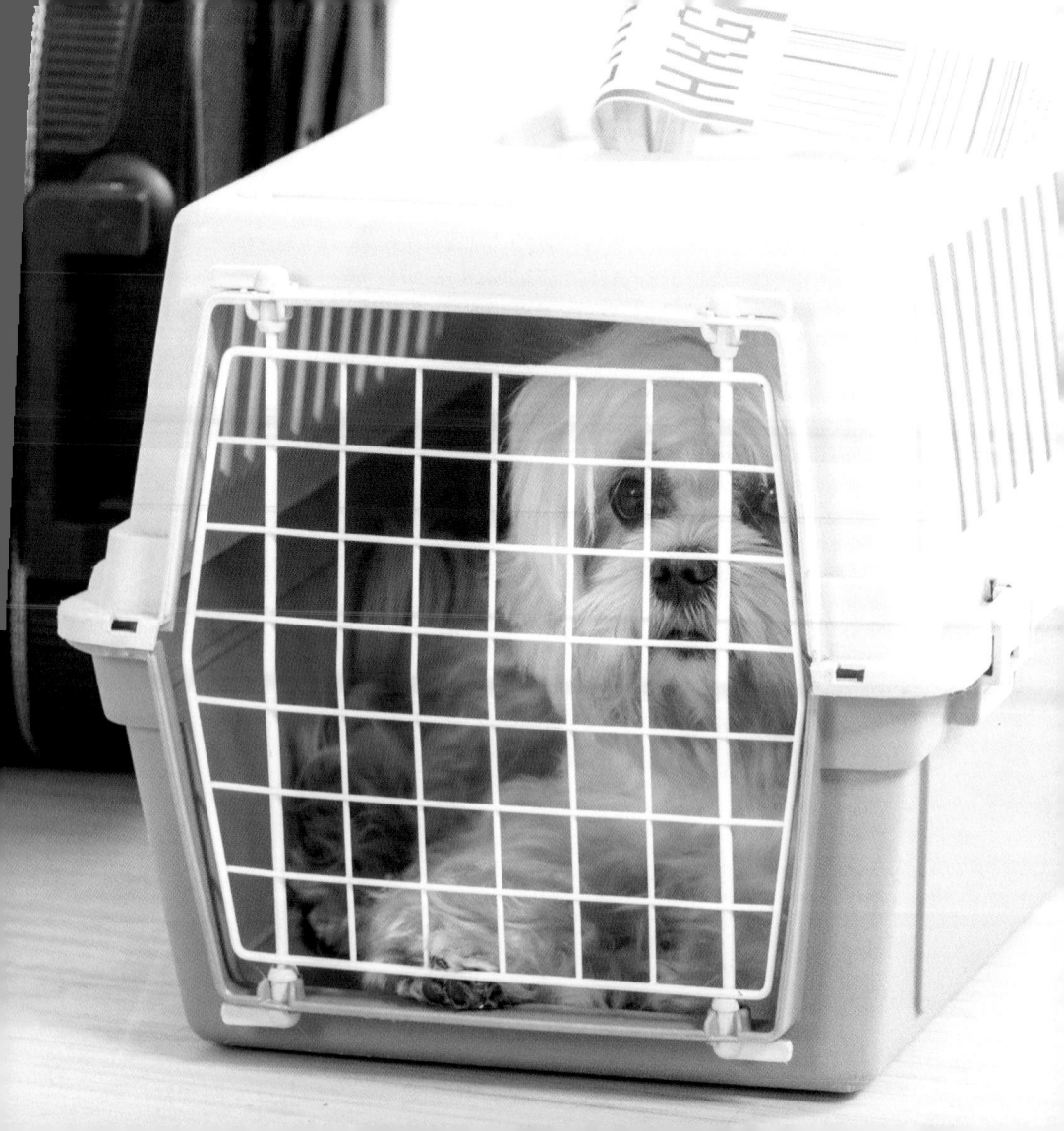

Stop feeling trapped by work travel...

...and start feeling the
wind in your hair!

File away that frustrating paperwork...

...and open the next chapter of your life!

Cut the cord on long conference calls...

...and dial in to fun!

Turn off boring busywork....

...and turn up the heat
on your hobbies!

Hang up the hard hat...

...and pick up your nine iron!

Decline the invite to another boring office party...

...and RSVP to the party of your life!

Put away those business suits...

...and put on your swimsuit!

Spend less time stuck in bad meetings...

...and spend more time
with your loved ones!

Avoid stop-and-go traffic on your commute...

...and stop and smell
the daisies instead!

Finally, it's time to stop living to work...

...and start living your

best retired life!

About the Author

Rex Barkington is a retired retriever and a very good boy. His hunting days are long behind him; in his retired life he is mostly focused on sniffing out treats. Rex spends his days napping on the golf course, napping by the pool, and napping on the beach. He lives in Florida.